The Revolver in the Hive

POETS
OUT LOUD

Elisabeth Frost, *series editor*

The Revolver in the Hive

Nicolas Hundley

Fordham
University Press
New York
2013

Library of Congress Cataloging-in-Publication Data

IIundlcy, Nicolas.
The revolver in the hive / Nicolas Hundley.—1st ed.
p. cm.— (Poets out loud)
ISBN 978-0-8232-5087-5 (cloth : alk. paper)
ISBN 978-0-8232-5088-2 (pbk. : alk. paper)
1. Loss (Psychology)—Poetry. 2. Grief—Poetry. I. Title.
PS3608.U54R48 2013
811'.6—dc23

2012036505

Printed in the United States of America
15 14 13 5 4 3 2 1
First edition

FOR EMILY

FOR JAMES

Contents

IV

The Revolver in the Hive

I

Death sets a Thing significant
The Eye had hurried by
Except a perished Creature

—EMILY DICKINSON

Gothic Novel

1.

I believe they believed what I said.

I said the vents whisper calculations
worth writing on your ankle.

As a watch on the counter, I said,
I imagined a boxcar inside.

I imagined I asked:

What about the revolver in the hive?
What about the thermos

propping open the book—
what book was it?

I imagined I knew this:

The streetlights turned into dots at the dawn.
The dots sounded like air conditioners

or they didn't sound like anything.

2.

I have invented this twitch
not thinking of you

on my gurney in the exhibit.

I have invented this:
A statue waiting all day long—

it starts to worry.

It worries a table with years missing from it
is no method for the sparrows.

It worries a fork in the swamp
is no refrain from the gauze.

In the swamp, I asked myself—
because I knew not whom to ask—

Did they mention a shawl?

3.

A lens is incapable of noise
even in that hut.

A noise darkens the hut.

That the urn wobbles within the hut—
not worth speculation.

It is not worth speculating the causes,
whether the asterisk caused

her to drop the lens in that urn.
I won't mention the urn made of wood,

the wooden urn.
I won't mention what this might entail.

I won't mention the noise
escaping from that urn.

Again

Again he conducts himself to the water's edge

to witness the profile of the distant islands
interrupting horizon, the smearing of sludge to sand.

Again he clutches the timepiece ruined in the electrical storm
from his youth and thinks of his youth,

and his skull starts to rattle, rattle with thought.
It rattles in thinking of the kin traveling on the water,

of the kin returning from the water, seeing them afterward
and not recognizing them afterward.

Again he inspects the driftwood, recites the psalms,
says his name backward. He offers the water

his embrace, he embraces the water, but the water
is difficult to grasp. So he strikes the water,

withholds his affection, but only momentarily.
He constructs a sundial in the sand, bellows out in loneliness,

hears his echo return from the water, feels consoled.
Again he curls up at the water's edge but cannot sleep,

sleeps, dreams about the pendulum of a clock.
He awakens to find the pendulum in his grasp,

casts it into the water, asks the water for it back, forgets.
Again he paces along the water's edge, speaks to the water,

speaks to his father in speaking to the water.
He invokes the man who one day walked past

the water's edge and into the water, the man
who was not to return from the water again.

The Blood You Let

The blood you let coagulated into amber. You enlisted leeches, siphon, syringe—but still felt weak, foolish, transparent, bureaucratic, and, in the end, remained the infanta. You sought mirrors, gained mirrors, took on mirrors and the endless corridors they elicited. Thinking it might give window into your infirmity, we propped you opposite mirrors. You grew impatient, mutilated them. You wore magnets arranged about your person. You called for absolution, and, absolved, resolved to die outside the church. Your eyes toggled, flickered, failed to lock onto anything. You grew spotted, suffered bumps, a Braille networking your flesh. We took to stones, warmed the stones, configured them on your person. We solicited healers, who opened you up, peered around, and for this we paid them. They smeared you in balm, nearly embalmed you. They siphoned out your breath, replaced it with an air brewed from ash and tar. They sent for tubes, for a length of tubing, and at this I had to intervene.

They

They—wrinkly, famished, under-lit—they
had finished braiding, finished their braids.
They brought their hauls of bottle,
they brought their scarabs. They—
thatched with stubble, replacements—
they replaced my transistors, but the transition
enlisted years to complete.
Always they—with pushcarts
undermined with oxidation, their algorithms,
their jars of screws, screws
in their jaws. They—those who
tightened the ratchet, who ratcheted. They—
on the imported sea-rocks—excavated
the device, clambered around the device,
defiled the device. They scratched
and took turns scratching. They—
tethered to their buckets of clams—
they smelled of fuel. They inhabited
my parlor, made it their habitat. They—
duplicating, duplicated—set up shop, grew roots.
They gave out roots, ate roots. Always
with their sickness, sickness
of numbers. They brewed elixirs.
They drank them out of hollowed-out gourds,
gorged themselves. They—
with pulleys, with sacks of mud—
stole my mud. They lodged
their lodge into my hill.

The Ecclesiastic Office of the Bicycle

Ever since I took the bicycle to the temple, wheeled it into the temple, ushered the bicycle down the aisle, past the pews frequented by rodent and fugitive, placed the bicycle at the altar, altered it with the bicycle, it has been the temple of the bicycle. And soon others began to enter the temple, to trample one another to view the bicycle, to touch the bicycle, to kneel at it and share the air with the bicycle. It became the bicycle of the poor, the bicycle of the sick, and so grew unfit to ride. There was established the office of the bicycle, and sermons were delivered on the bicycle. Even the skeptics, the zealots, the devout, those branding the bicycle false idol, those refusing to idolize it, idolized it. O bicycle arrayed with rust, calibrated for laceration! O bicycle inherited by way of debt, stolen and recovered from the river! Bicycle I shared with the widow who cleaned fish, bicycle I lost in my youth.

The Mourners

In the middle of the night the mourners collected,
collected on our lawn. They tested our locks,

pried open our entrance, gained entrance.
They peopled our rooms, took stock,

accounted for our plugs, what we had
with which to populate the plugs.

They tracked in mud, muddied up the place,
placed their trash where they saw fit.

They rattled our cages, our cages of fowl.
They infiltrated our provisions, provisioned them out.

Some of the mourners were family, others
familiar as a pet is familiar, returning years later

stitched up from experimentation.
They tethered us to our grief

when all we wanted was to flee the grief.
They siphoned out our grief in the event our grief

should be reconstituted into another.
They quoted from their volumes,

took shelter, though no shelter was offered.
They spent all night ranting in the yard.

Sonnet

My theory is broken.
My robe may be beautiful but it weighs a ton.
A newspaper is draining down the steps
to where a man is planting a gate.
At the gate, the chariot sits there
like some kind of joke.
My robe is brass and I never remove it.
I pause on the steps overlooking the tournament
to where a man is weighing plants
in a tent behind the trumpets.
My newspaper is broken.
Is the pain some kind of joke?
My chariot may be broken but it is beautiful—
the unrelenting steps.

Portrait with Piano and Axe

The widow resumes her seat at the piano in her room.
And though she is unfamiliar with the terrain of the piano,

the piano accommodates her grip, her meanderings
across its keys. And though she is gripped by fear,

though she fears the piano, in the sheen of the piano
she finds condolence, a chandelier, a puddle

without a counterpart outside the reflection,
an axe. She traces the reflection of the axe

to its reference point in the room. She grips the axe,
as once she gripped the piano, introduces it

into the threshold of the piano. She weeps,
but out of joy. She opens the piano to view its insides.

She explores its insides with her tongue. She catches
her reflection in the mirror, does not recognize herself,

moves at random but is preempted by the figure
in its pool. She admires the taxidermy,

the portraiture of her progeny splayed
across the walls. And though the sound of her song

still echoes, still she returns to the piano.
And though she yearns to leave the room,

she is under the piano's spell. She regains her seat
before the piano, elicits a caterwaul from its hobbled hull.

Tooth and Blur

I had become the grief. I gnashed and bit
at the air. My features corroded, and I grew
new ones—fangs, fur, claw. I was all tooth and blur.
I sputtered, barked. I soiled myself, owned the stench.
They were forced to watch me perform these crimes.
I contorted, revolted them with my contortions.
I bared my ribs, emptied the contents
of my mind—stores of guilt and humiliation—
as though they were the contents of my stomach.
I polluted the air with invectives.
I had tenure as resident to their skulls.

Once

You dressed wounds, were the wound-dresser. You invented, and your inventions will go on to outlive you. You had performed, been applauded, forgotten. You lived indoors for years at a time unflinchingly. You had offspring—you procreated—and as your progeny progressed, they distanced themselves from you. You raised fowl, caged fowl, sold fowl, for which you were rewarded handsomely. You collected rainwater in tins, you trained your tins toward the rain. You had acquired disease, disorder, a catalog of symptoms without corresponding affliction. You had gone on listening to the transistor radio into the half-light, half-heard someone's recipe for elixir, had half an inkling to realize it in your vat. You had primed the well, portioned out well-water, and this is the appreciation you get. You had traveled, traveled with the parcel, which, in your transport, dozed away its years. You had erected the shelter, took shelter, sheltered others, neglected the shelter. You had fallen asleep, had slept, but in sleeping, siphoned a portion of your dream into reality as you woke. You had just as quickly tired of it, attempted to reinsert it back into dream, failed. Emerging from sleep unscathed countless times, you would always return to sleep again.

II

Mirrors and copulation are
abominable, for they multiply
the number of mankind.

—JORGE LUIS BORGES

The Duplications

When I witness the duplications—the perverse breeding that
transpires in their factories—
I fail at computation. I swivel, sputter, lose my functions.
When I witness the duplications, when I see them
there—duplicating—
I scarce have any arousal. When they go about duplicating and
they don't try to hide it,
I freeze in the container I am in and puzzle.
I retch, take the wrench and hoist it. I threaten them with it.
When I witness them—their exoskeletons, their skeletal
appearance, attenuated flesh—I resort to convulsions.
When I watch the acts they perform on conveyor belts, I react
poorly, have an inkling to reenact them on my own.
When I see what poor hygiene they exhibit, I recoil, feel my
intestines coil up inside me.
When I see their numbers in rank and file vanish into the
horizon, I attempt to elicit the illusion
of greater numbers for myself. I enlist a system of mirrors
toward this end.
When I imagine their progeny—the product of exponential
facsimiles—I imagine them disfigured,
missing some key component from the transference. I become
agitated and, in turn, instigate agitation upon others.
I lose my attentions, stop manning the board, bore into a
corner and hide.
When I consider their alchemy, their androgyny, their
implications, their lack of impotence, I grieve. I reset
and emerge refueled and envious. When I study their
structures, their inner-structures, their inner-
workings, the enigma of their operations—I fail at explanation.

When I subject them to my proddings, test their properties and
prioritize my findings—I find it difficult to formulate
conclusions.
When I witness them, their competitive procreation—I
provoke them. I spit on them, hurl insults,
but only lose regard for myself in so doing. I give up and
marvel.

Fathering the Machine

I filled it with stones because stones gave it weight. Sponging it with a tenderness reserved for flesh, I elicited only rust. I could tell by its cheerful expression it was too stupid to be of any use. I rocked it in my arms and, unable to shoulder its girth, buckled. I dressed it up, put it in a dress, a bonnet; alternately, an ascot, tailored it a boxy blazer. I made it atomic, anatomic, altruistic, removed that glitch, gave it a disposal. I gave it a stutter, a stammer, an oral fixation, a trick lens, one appendage shorter than the other, each successive appendage suffering from the same affliction. I gave it a gear box, a fuse box, a black box, a glove box, a wallet, a prophylactic. I gave it fear, fear and a public education, humility and ironic detachment. I gave it a name. I renamed it, rotated its nomenclature based on whim. I retooled it, untooled it, couldn't remember the original tooling. I treasured it, teased it, raised it by hand, undermined its self-worth through manipulation and emasculation. I touched it affectionately, rarely, inappropriately. I thought it to so resemble me in its making, I went about its unmaking.

That's When I Was Thinking

When first I noticed the ridges in my hands,
I was on a picnic in the Ozarks.
I was eating a root.
The local creatures were all very courteous,
and the woods—full of little sticks.
That's when a moon spanning several feet
began to shudder and gleam.
Someone said it was an intricate chasm
filled with fossils of extinct creatures.
But before I got to "moon"
in the dictionary, I came upon "deprivation."
The lawn is deprived of rain,
and indeed it was.
The harbor planes tied to the bamboo docks.
They bobbed back and forth on pontoons.
And from my hill, I noticed
where their wings were still wet
from the particle baths they call "The Rain."
Some of the planes were spotted. Others wrinkled.

There Was No Wind

Insects loiter over the tarmac.
Chauffeured on forklifts, the girls arrive—
they have come to tell us about the houseboats.
"Houseboats," they say.
Everyone is pumping gas.
The carpenter carries a bucket of water,
he never says why.
He never says "soon" in a sentence.
I want to tell him I bought too many lottery tickets.
I want to tell him something
about a dulcimer and a hubcap,
but I bet he wouldn't listen.
He's too busy at the bonsai exhibit
positioning himself in a slab of sun.
Now I may be easy to impress science-wise,
but I hear accordions in the distance.
I thought I might recline.

Their Instruments

In order to calculate the precise moment of your death, you donated yourself to their instruments. You fed yourself to them, and it was years before you were digested. You received only printouts—a Tourette's of symbols—as souvenir. Their instruments radiated, irradiated you, and now you're prone to glow. You gave yourself to their instruments, which passed judgment on you. For some time you retained evidence of them in your inner-organs, your inner-ear, the seventh circle of your digestive tract. You found their instruments cold, impersonal, given to blip—their answer to a belch. You donated yourself to their instruments, in whose possession you remained until they had expired all readings, left you tender and unemployed.

The Thoughts That Are the Byproduct of Your Existence

The thoughts that are the byproduct of your existence come of
age
in the cask of your skull. They collude with rot, mutate, evolve,
devolve,
revolve in mid-air before collapsing into puddle.
They grow subversive, hatch plots for domain of your person.

The thoughts that are the byproduct of solving the equation
spread out in rings.
They cannot be poured down the drain. They require licensed
transport.
They burn to be included in the equation and live forever in
the equation.

The thoughts that are the byproduct of performing the prayer
subvert the prayer.
They attempt to proselytize your lobe. They lecture your glands,
and your immune system can't keep up.
They refuse to break down, decompose, dissolve, drown.
They protrude, test the boundaries of your brain, stretch your
helmet into new dimensions.

The thoughts that are the byproduct of your self-loathing can
be hewn into figurines.
They freeze well, bare their ribs through their skin.
They mature in electrical storms, are informed by legacies of
guilt and atmospheric interference.

The thoughts that are the byproduct of exercising the gland
arrive with auras.
They need relief, so you commission a well into your skull.
You invite speculation, lease out your person.

The thoughts that are the byproduct of the ritual default to
panic.
They are easily indoctrinated into the cause, causing them to
convulse with fanaticism and purpose.
They rail against the state, decry the state, state their hatred for
it, and the state holds you responsible.

The thoughts that are the byproduct of developing the antidote
can be repurposed for sustenance.
They eat their own, devour themselves, which only increases
their concentration.
They rarely exhibit gratitude, gravitate toward darker matters,
fixate, get into the atmosphere.

Altercations with the Maharajah

They love their Braille, the French.
They are all contortionists in some respect.
They use an intricate network of pulleys to purchase their
gouda.
Gouda is a cheese drunk on tantric reverie.
Gouda is the name of a bird I once owned.
Often I see him, perched on the branch of a gingko tree.
The gingko tree, he tells me, loses all its leaves within two
hours.
The gingko tree, long thought extinct, was rediscovered in a
monastery garden
when the French arrived, wearing buttons.
The monks were wearing sombreros and sipping martinis.
They were contortionists in their own right, lost in a tantric
can-can.
They were gazing at the petroglyphs through a telescope.
Petroglyphs have even been found on the inside of bathroom
stalls.
Upon their return the French carried cocoons—
from one hatched a bird named Gouda.
Gouda is narcoleptic and prone to flying drunk.
Occasionally, I must retrieve him from his branch with pulleys.
At such times, after he's had a number of martinis,
Gouda points into the telescope at the Sombrero Galaxy.
He says the Sombrero Galaxy says something in Braille,
the Braille something in French.

The Ill

The ill (the virus-clad), the weak (the deficient of will) knitted (gave way to) a pantheon of doilies to apply to (festoon) the steel casings (the fuselages) of our vaults (our lockboxes, our black boxes, our jewelry boxes, the boxes for our boxing gloves, our boxes of undergloves), under which an undisclosed wealth of treasures (the aforementioned) remained submerged (draped in doilies). The expanse (the meteor fields) invited our journey. Our journey became replete with creatures (fin-featured) and creature-comforts (adding machines). One of the adding machines (Gabriel) gave off (secreted) a rambling of German secrets serving as the basis for our ethical framework (waistcoats). This came in handy in the trials of fortitude (dispute with fellow man) laid out before us in our travels through the provinces (our inner turmoils), but not with the landmines.

Allegory of the Well-Dressed Man

A man dressed like a man. Another man mannishly dressed. One man mistaken for a man. Another man dressed like a woman. A womanly man, who has been so ever since the womb. A man lost, distraught, desperate, hauling strands of kelp. A man hallucinating, broadcasting thoughts, thinking them, and just as soon the thoughts giving wing and offending others. A man calibrating the device, devising a method to engineer wealth and calibrate a life of leisure away from the device. A man tallying stars, losing track of them, starting over. A man tethered to his desk. A man heir to the atrocities, inheriting them, and in his possession their legacy only growing more atrocious. A man acting as progenitor, progeny unfolding from him into the horizon. A man authoring the manual, devoting his life to the manual, which is soon rendered obsolete by a new model of his muse. A man ostracized, but able to entertain himself sufficiently in his exile. A man manning the board. A man a conduit for visions, a vessel for them, who becomes possessive, withholds them from others. A man defeated, but distinctive in his defeat.

Two Poems

1.

The antiquarian uncovers a pendulum
to a grandfather clock in a pile of typewriters,

engine belts, and vacuum cleaners in the junkyard

at the end of the street. A lit bulb swings
across a broom closet in the laboratory

where the alchemist stirs silver into the prescription vats.
Upstairs, a widow uses a blue leaf as a bookmark.

The electric fence hums in the dusk as the caretaker insists
that the scarecrow dangles atop the tire heap because

"The gawk of the magpie is a muffler rusting."

2.

"This pocket watch is a pathological liar,"
thinks the old man waiting for yesterday's train,

which arrives today only a breeze through the platform.

Two farmers harmonize in the town square—
"Almost the crops are at the appropriate aperture."

A gold tooth gleaming in the sun the only evidence.

The carved bell of the steeple echoes down the alley
where the map-maker drafts the jagged rim of the canyon.

Birds peck through puddles in the dirt road,
moisture curdles into storm clouds in the far sky.

Public Record

How we engineered rain. How we bludgeoned the harvest. How the shelter eroded. How we eked out survival in the trees. How we used the trees for our livelihood. How we peopled the valley, abandoned the valley, repeopled it. How industry became acquainted with the valley. How the valley industrialized. How thought became its industry. How institutions emerged as our factories. How age eluded us. How we eluded age. How the mechanism arrived in our sleep. How species happened. How we learned the science of the lake. How we submerged the town.

III

The most merciful thing in the world, I think, is the inability of the human mind to correlate all its contents.

—H. P. LOVECRAFT

Etc.

&

There were doctors—doctors of teeth,
doctors of feet, doctors of brains, doctors
of the beasts. There were doctors concealing
their perversions in their profession.
There were doors—always doors—and the twisted
lights waiting behind them. There were
underwater lights, atmospheric lights, the lights
populating the mind of a cat. There were few choices.
One could be a soldier, a sailor, a widow, a leader
of men, an inventor. There were
weathers and the predictions of weathers,
and we only confused them in our minds.
There was a science smuggled inside us
that turned blue during the eclipse.

&

I kept sod in spools, spooled sod,
trafficked in it, paved my parcel with it, ushered in
new possibilities in sod. I went about unsleeping,
excelled at it for days. I alternated unsleeping and hyper-
sleeping until my glands were permanently damaged.
I funneled elixir down my gullet, took it down
and gave it chase with a brew eliciting its regurgitation.
I studied the evacuant, the puddle, its colonies
of half-dissolved matter and pockets of iridescence.
My insides writhed. I lost my functions. I rested
in the tender embrace of a satellite dish,
unaware of the transmissions passing through me.
I ruthlessly slept, and in sleeping, disrupted the feed
from the satellite circling above.

&

The throngs of unkempt sailors, throngs
of the lice-ridden, the calcium-caked,
the odorous—we went about scrounging bamboo.
We kept captives. We entertained captives,
capsized them, offered them condiments,
sedated them, and piled them in a room.
We kept cattle, livestock, larvae, lichens—
and our wealth multiplied exponentially
with their numbers. We organized
in the ravine. We collected eggs, bled the livestock.
We made sausage from the blood, blood pudding,
bloodied our clothes in the process. We procured
several diseases as if on purpose.
We grew shiny in the half-light, fiercely aware.

&

The blast site had cooled. They were raking it
for clues, dragging their nets through it,
coming up empty, searching for more promising ash
in which to try their luck. Sub-
sonic frequencies lured me into sleep.
The steely taste of teeth. My skull had a live
feed, was being fed melodies that loitered in the fore
-front of my brain, unable to navigate
the labyrinth of circuits to rest in storage.
A river appeared. Now my plot is cloven.
Men clad in lab coats are poring over the cross
section of a tree, counting its rings,
placing wagers on the age of the tree.
Who summoned the courier of organs?

&

To submerge your hand in theocracy
results in chronic night terrors. Whole societies
of bacteria in my veins. My arm devolved
into wires, my entrails trailed off
into a network of tubes. You ignored the ingot
despite the fury you had ignited over it,
quickly returned to your enterprise
of administering rust. One man was working
with soot. It suited him. Others were in the bushes,
developing their tolerance to poison.
There they were, issuing from the background,
cutting gruesome figures. There
they were, soliciting the past for artifacts.
The death of my left arm was completely unforeseen.

&

Where you counted stones, trafficked stones,
bred stones. Where I swallowed
insects, felt them grow frantic in my throat
and extinguish in my stomach.
Where you mostly wept, partly grieved, moaned,
bled. Where I arranged the plans, rolled up the plans,
placed them in a canister until they could be enacted.
Where I sent the canister into the river with aim
to intercept it downstream. Where you entered the trance,
grew entranced, fell under its spell,
shared your visions. Where I grunted, learned
the grunt, perfected it, demonstrated it.
Where the pipe discharged. Where ground
was broken. Where I buried the noise in a jar.

&

I was purchasing teeth. I was browsing
from an array of teeth, through the catalogs
of those who trafficked in teeth.
Where did they get the teeth?
I was troubled by my glands. They gave me grief,
so I fed them electricity, smeared them
with mineral, attempted to mitigate them
through wraps, rinse, extraction.
The others were frolicking in the ashes.
This left them ashen. They alternated on the organ,
then donated their organs, repented, attempted
to reobtain them. I was amused by this.
Then I was pained. I collapsed the accordion, broke it
in so doing, sold it for scrap, hear it in my dreams.

&

They're exploring the sewers by torch-light,
torturing themselves to solve their way out.
I stood poised at the receiver with a net,
positioned to capture the transmission
as it hurled out. I was aware of the algorithms
dictating my actions but unable to argue
with them. I purchased the worms
only after painstaking research—I would need
just the right ones, took great pains
not to misselect them, those worms.
They found my ancestor incarcerated
in a block of ice, undertook to thaw him out.
They managed to clone a cloud and unleash it
into our sky, awarding us a redundant shade.

&

I held the insect even as it panicked
in my grasp. I created a chamber
with both hands and felt it stir and puzzle
at the vestibule I made. I collected others,
inserted them into jars and gave you
the most breathtaking examples.
I introduced them to captivity, to which they
responded miserably. I transported the waste,
had nowhere to store it, wasted
hours circling with it. I ingested the substance
eliciting glow from my entrails,
made my entrails glow, thereafter had window
into my inner-workings. I swallowed
clock parts just to see their silhouettes.

&

The bacteria inhabiting my blood
developed methods to police my blood,
to administer justice. I awoke to inspect
what had accumulated in the net
during the night. Despite your urgings,
I aggravated the wound, wound up infecting it,
and now its ache prefigures amputation.
I walked the path culminating in factory, saw them
there, clamoring around the vats,
pouring in numbers, stirring them to elicit grotesque
new integers. I laid blame, distributed blame,
did so liberally, liberated the blame from those
deserving of it, stole the blame, for soon
there wouldn't be enough to go around.

&

They were running algorithms, testing algorithms,
drunk on equation and reduced to lawlessness
in the form of subversive theorems.
My arm—rivers of code and mutilated
antibodies that had started to glow—
started to glow. There were several cubes
littered about, which I kicked and in kicking
earned some consolation. I heard a mutilated
bugle multiplying into fanfare at the ceremony.
It was a ceremony of some gravity,
a ceremony dedicated to gravity. They
had been set free to prod at the equipment
and us. They smelled, smelt, spoke in sputters,
stammered, locked onto staccato. They fed on air.

&

Heretical machines enacting misdeeds,
fulfilling the equation. The saintly demeanor
of other machines originates in programming.
Distemper found me there, in the reeds.
There were creatures enacting eggs,
oligarchs under the influence of elixir
growing despondent, discovering the consolations
of war. I entered the shed, shed my cloak
of daylight at its threshold. In its darkness
I decoded several objects. There was
the smell of iron, a rotting hulk. There were jars
of the remedy, discarded candelabra,
possessions. There was a segment
of banister banished from the house.

&

I brokered for fuel and in so doing fueled
others' dislike for me, gave them fuel
for their impersonations, which I can attest
offer astute renderings. I have a prosthetic frontal lobe,
which registers as ringing in my ears when I sneeze.
My posture is broken. I postulate it's due
to the meteor showers, to ducking debris hurled from
the heavens—decommissioned satellites and astral trash
breaking orbit and returning to Earth. I incarcerated
the cry as it developed inside me, where
now it ricochets, brokers unceasingly for release.
I withstand several waves of sleep passing over me
before resigning myself to its power.
Later, I awake in a nest of wires.

&

You hauled the busted statue in a sack,
solicited assistance to solder its limbs back on,
balked at my suggestion that—shattered—
it had acquired an air of antiquity it otherwise
couldn't attain. Hauling your cargo as such left you
exhausted, and in order to restore your faculties,
you secured a measure of sleep by the well.
When you awoke, the well water had grown polluted.
The villagers blamed your dreams,
obliged you to dig a new well.
You suffered discolorations, gave yourself
over to splotches without resistance.
You had fallen into rot. Your rot
was examined, absolution outsourced.

&

I was haunted by one of the humors
but couldn't tell which. My glands
were producing an excess of dark matter,
New Criticism, abstract reasoning,
smut. So they swapped out a cartridge,
and now I'm deficient in pattern recognition.
I donated myself to the hypnotism. They
hypnotized me in order to harvest my memories.
They resorted to siphon, syringe, a system
of pulleys, but still they wouldn't surface.
I repaired to the place of my birth.
I was wearing a homing device.
I gave off blips, was given to blip. I saw a pope
appear by the shed, easily shed the vision.

IV

Once an angry man dragged
his father along the ground
through his own orchard.
"Stop!" cried the groaning old
man at last, "Stop! I did not
drag my father beyond this
tree."

—GERTRUDE STEIN

What the Wires Feed

Dear toxic lake. Dear sheen on the lake,
flammable lake. Dear lockjaw, jaw rusted shut,
jaw of the corrosive hinge. Dear braincloud.
Dear toxins. Dear limb caught in the trap.
Dear wires, what the wires feed. Dear negative.
Dear negated verb. Dear pipe, network
of pipes. Dear inner-ear, inner-organs.
Dear entrails. Dear transfusion. In my veins
you sing another. Dear father inside the urn.
Dear ash. Dear dark inside the urn, darker still.

Widow in the Labyrinth

She follows a single wall for years, traces its meanderings informed by perpendicular angles and perverted logic. Each day she awakens in the labyrinth, lacks recollection of how she arrived. Birds refuse to instruct her to attain exit. She hauls a sack filled with the limbs of statues. Frost has been administered around her eyes. You arc the widow in the labyrinth. You are the walls and the cracks in the walls, the gravel on the ground. You were widowed by the labyrinth.

When We Were Impressionable

At a time when the fork
was our only instrument,
I gathered the bulbs in shallow nests
to sell on the side of the road.

This is how it starts, you said—
the sun's bands stroking a phlox in the field;
the bird bath bubbles in the back yard.
Nothing embalmed for days on end.

Lightning came, lightning left,
leaving the traffic lights in disarray.
The drawer too in disarray—
emptied of emblems.

And the banging on the pipes?
Not the reason I swivel my head.
The sky begins to fold over on itself—
this is but one indication of night.

Burial Practice

They strike out at dawn when the tide is out
to deposit him miles from shore. They weigh
him down, slide stones into his pockets, sew coins
into the lining of his suit. They pour molasses
down his throat, laden him with chains, siphon
the air from his lungs. They shave him
as though he were a swimmer, remove what hair
remains on his head. They don't bother
to embalm him, for this will be accomplished by the sea.
They offer him their hymns, their verses. They
bring wreaths of driftwood for this man
who is wizened, weathered, himself driftwood.

Inventing the Code

We had brewed the code and kept it
in captivity for a number of years.
The code—atonal, beautiful, apocryphal—
we refined with our instruments
of science. We coated it in jewels
we had foraged in the near dark.
We buried it in the unyielding earth
for winter, harvested it, cuddled it
like kin parceled back from war,
sponged it, reinserted the capacitor.
The code emerged from our dialects
of distrust and nostalgia. We each
contributed to the code. My contributions—
"hobbyhorse," "hoarfrost," "Himalaya."
We needed the code to carry out the irrigation,
the irrigation of the root, to refer
to the stitches without direct reference
to the stitches, to the rain and to the rash
we received from the rain. We needed
the code to guard our secrets from them—
them locksmiths, them plumbers, them
merchants, merchants of frost and plastic
who wanted to consolidate our weather
into whatever weather their dome would bless.

Braintree

The druid writing
the instruction manual

on the random
number generator

is a bleeder.

In the crater
owing to an asteroid

dispatched
some centuries past,

I found
the amulet delicately

distorted
with refraction,

prisming
the refinery's plume.

Then in the closet
of the mother

of my mother,

the length of pipe
I encountered

blindly

reaching into
its dark.

String Theory

Some sort of baroque cascaded through the window.
The air was full of violence,
but you wouldn't know it.
A cathedral grew out of my arm.
I tended to it with the extract of root,
then I rooted it out with a switch.
Then I buried the fucker at the riverbank.
Then it grew into a cathedral.
They said it was a baroque cathedral.
I took communion there, before it grew too dangerous.
It was full of chalk outlines, the outlines
of habits and rosary beads—
the result of a baroque violence. Thereafter,
I took my communion at the river, by the portion of the river
where thc river oxbowed. I buried the rosary
at the riverbank. Then I broke the river.

What Remains

What remains has already been picked through,
pored over, subjected to scrutiny, scavenged
for organs, scrap parts, copper wiring,
scanned for salvageable thoughts,
but none were found worth salvaging.
What remains is mostly ash, teeth, capacitors,
undissolved medication. What remains
is difficult to handle, evades rake, broom, suction.
It won't suffer any sack, its dimensions
inappropriate for coffin or urn. It goes
unnoticed, ignored, dismissed, forgotten. What remains
awaits someone to claim it, whether widow or wind.

When the Device Fails

When the device you invented has failed you, brings shame upon you, humiliates you, when it becomes a conglomeration of malfunction and miscalculation, dump it down the well. When it implicates you in its programming, when its manufacture bears your signature and its existence will serve as a reminder of your failure, find a hole in the earth to dispose of it. Say a few words before you do. Commemorate the occasion. Wait until the sky is gauzed with clouds, after it's been bled of light, when the device suspects nothing. Drag it through the dirt, for it should not be sent into the earth unacquainted with earth. Bludgeon it with weapons requiring no moving parts. Disfigure it, nurse it, spit on it, cradle it, weep into it. Tell it your fears, your true stance on the hereafter, for hereafter it will have no one with whom to share your disclosure. Ask if it requires absolution and, if so, administer it yourself, even if you lack the authority.

Gallery of Fathers

One with bloated digits. One in the ducts.
One dissolving into shadow,
enshrouded in the shadow of the shed.
One demonstrating the saw. One sawing.
One threading, sharpening, shouting
into the jar. One fattening himself
before the window. One gloved.
One repairing the sink. One failed,
a failure, trolling the porch.
One radiating with stink. One a fraud,
fraudulent, flatulent, sickened from stew.
One repairing himself by the light. One
clutching at his unspooling garb, grabbing at it,
but in vain. One with offerings of rocks.
One offering rocks to the pond. One who traps.
One who visits the traps periodically,
inspects the traps, traps their location
in his memory and later accounts for them
on his rounds. One who perches.
One perched on the roof.

Meadow Vacant

And then I took the urn

after it accumulated years in the closet,
after it had taken on an iridescence
indigenous to the dark.

Beneath a sky frequented by satellites,
I took it to the cricket's mechanical strum,

through forests not calibrated
for foot traffic or flashlight,

down several slopes angled toward
no particular constellation.

When my grip had finally expired,
I took a seat on an obsolete sundial
in a meadow vacant of meaning.

A barn half-burnt down
disinterestedly kept watch.

From the ruins, a pile of stones
urged me to fill the urn with stones,
to send it into the river;

the weathervane to dump it down the well.

Instead, as dawn bruised the horizon,
I opened the urn and poured out the song,

which, in the gathering wind, traveled
past the silhouettes of the telephone wires

and the silo at the field's fringe,
past the highway leading to the city of noise,

past the city of noise.

Notes and Acknowledgments

Poems in this book originally appeared in the following publications:

Conduit: "Gothic Novel" and "That's When I Was Thinking"
Crazyhorse: "Fathering the Machine" and "The Blood You Let"
FIELD: "What the Wires Feed" and "Widow in the Labyrinth"
Gulf Coast: "The Mourners"
LIT: "Meadow Vacant"
Massachusetts Review: "The Duplications"
POOL: "The Ecclesiastic Office of the Bicycle" and "Once"
Salt Hill: "Altercations with the Maharajah"
Seattle Review: "When We Were Impressionable"
Verse: "Again" and "They"

Page 1: The Emily Dickinson quotation is from the poem "Death Sets a Thing Significant" (360).
Page 15: The Jorge Luis Borges quotation is from the story "Tlön, Uqbar, Orbis Tertius," translated by Andrew Hurley.
Page 25: The poem "Altercations with the Maharajah" uses words and phrases from *Moulin Rouge!* (2001), directed by Baz Luhrmann and written by Baz Luhrmann and Craig Pearce.
Page 31: The H. P. Lovecraft quotation is from the story "The Call of Cthulhu."
Page 49: The Gertrude Stein quotation is from *The Making of Americans.*

Thank you to my mother, to my family and friends, and to those who provided encouragement and feedback on these poems, especially James Tate and Dara Wier. Thank you to the editors who previously published these poems. Thank you to Elisabeth Frost and everyone at Fordham University Press.

POETS OUT LOUD PRIZE WINNERS

Amy Sara Carroll
Fannie + Freddie: The Sentimentality of Post–9/11 Pornography

Nicolas Hundley
The Revolver in the Hive
EDITOR'S PRIZE

Julie Choffel
The Hello Delay

Michelle Naka Pierce
Continuous Frieze Bordering Red
EDITOR'S PRIZE

Leslie C. Chang
Things That No Longer Delight Me

Amy Catanzano
Multiversal

Darcie Dennigan
Corinna A-Maying the Apocalypse

Karin Gottshall
Crocus

Jean Gallagher
This Minute

Lee Robinson
Hearsay

Janet Kaplan
The Glazier's Country

Robert Thomas
Door to Door

Julie Sheehan
Thaw

Jennifer Clarvoe
Invisible Tender